the Yiddish are coming!

written by
Robyn M. Cohen

illustrated by
Robyn B. Rousso

LONGSTREET PRESS
Atlanta, Georgia

To my parents, Edie and Larry, and the rest of my family and friends, for all of their support and for believing in me. And a most special thanks to my Grandma Lakie, who introduced me to the wonderful world of Yiddish — without her, there would be no book.

— **Robyn Melinda Cohen**

I dedicate this book to my husband, Tony, and my son, Graham, whose love and laughter continually inspire me. Thanks to my family and friends for their love and support, to my mother, Corrine, who spoke Yiddish with love, and to my father, Morris, who shared his passion for art.

— **Robyn Beth Rousso**

Published by LONGSTREET PRESS, INC.,
a subsidiary of Cox Newspapers,
a division of Cox Enterprises, Inc.
2140 Newmarket Parkway, Suite 118
Marietta, Georgia 30067

Text copyright © 1994 by Robyn M. Cohen
Illustrations copyright © 1994 by Robyn B. Rousso

Printed in the United States of America
1st printing, 1994
Library of Congress Catalog Number 97-77583
ISBN: 1-56352-169-5

This book was printed by Dickinson Press Inc., Grand Rapids, Michigan.
Cover and book design by Robyn B. Rousso

Preface

For those of us growing up in the South, speaking Yiddish was quite a novelty. And as we got older, we realized this wonderful, tradition-filled language was dying out — especially with the twenty- and thirty-something crowds. So we came up with the idea for this book as a fun and imaginative way for people of all ages to learn some Yiddish to help keep this colorful language alive.

The book is designed in an A-to-Z format with each letter coming to life with a hilariously zany Jewish character. We did our best to capture parts of the Yiddish language and some Jewish humor as well. We have had a good time poking fun at all kinds of people, but the satire is not meant to be taken seriously in any way. Our book is intended solely to teach and entertain in a light-hearted manner. And if someone, anyone, learns a new Yiddish word to use and share with friends, then we've done our part to preserve this wonderfully expressive language.

You'll find both pronunciation and vocabulary meanings for every word at the foot of each page. Plus, there's a complete glossary in the back to help explain some of the more literal translations. So have fun, learn, and enjoy! You may be surprised how many words you do or don't know!

"A" is for Arnold the **alter kaker**, who lived in an **awngepatshket** house. When he ate he got so **awngebluzen**, it's no wonder he never found a spouse.

---

alter kaker (OLL-ter Cock-er) crotchety old man · awngepatshket (AWN-ge-potch-ket) cluttered · awngebluzen (AWN-ge-bluz-in) bloated

"B" is for Bertha the **bubbe**, who believed the world was **bakakt**. "I wouldn't give people **bubkes** for all their **bubbe Maises**," said Bertha. "Oy, some people... they're such a crock!"

bubbe (BU-bee) grandmother · bakakt (BAH-cocked) all fouled up · bubkes (BUB-kess) beans, nothing · bubbe maises (BU-bee My-suhs) silly stories

"C" is for Charlie the **chazir**, who put up with a lot of **chazerai** in his life. "Oy, the **chutzpa** it takes," cried Charlie, "just to deal with my **cockamamy** wife!"

chazir (KHOZ-zer) pig, greedy person • chazerai (Khoz-zair-EYE) "crap" • chutzpa (KHOOTS-pah) nerve, gall • cockamamy (cock-a-may-me) mixed-up

"D" is for Dorris the **dray kop**, who dreamed of singing in a famous Rock & Roll Band. "She **drein a Kawps** me so," complained her mother. "**Oy,** I tell you this much... my daughter, she's no Streisand."

dray kop (DRAY-cup) scatterbrain · drein a kawps (DRAY-in A Cups) annoys ·
Oy (like "boy") Oh!

"E" is for Esther the **edel**, who spent every

Sunday with her **bubbe** Lilly. "Eat a little **eppes**," her **bubbe**

would plead; "try my **gefilte fish**, it won't be **ek velt** if you don't like it, silly."

edel (AY-d'l) gentle person · bubbe (BU-bee) grandmother · eppes (E P - piss) something ·
gefilte fish (ge-FILL-teh fish) fishcakes · ek velt (ECK velt) the end of the world

"F" is for funny Fayge, who always got so *farmihsht*. When she went out she got so *farblunjet* and *farklempt*, she could never remembered if she'd *pished!*

farmihsht (far-MISHED) mixed up · farblunjet (far-BLWAN-jit) bewildered.
farklempt (FAH-klempt) distressed · pished (like "fished") urinated

"G" is for Gloria, whose boyfriend was a **goy.** "Oy gottenyu!" exclaimed Gloria's mother; "she's got so much **gelt,** I'm just not **gefelt,** what if he's a **ganef** of a boy?"

goy (like "boy") non-jew · Oy gottenyu! (OY GAWT-en-yew) "Oh, dear God!" · gelt (like "felt") money · gefelt (GUH-felt) satisfied · ganef (GON-iff) a thief

"H" is for Hymie the *haimisher* hermit, who lived out in *hotzenklotz* with his cat. "I've got *hak un pak*," he told his mother. "So quit *hakn me a chainik* about this and that!"

haimisher (HAME-ish-er) warm • hotzenklotz (HOTS-in-klotz) the sticks • hak un pak (HOCK-un-pock) everything • hakn me a chainik (HOCK-in ME A CHAN-ick) to babble

"I" is for Irving, who spent all of his free time **in bod** at home. "A man of **iker** should never have an **ipish**," he explained; "otherwise he'll find himself very much alone."

in bod (In Bud) in the bath • iker (E- care) substance.
ipish (IP- ish) bad odor

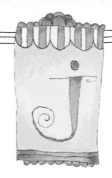

"J" is for Jacob the **jokenik**, who worked

for Miss Jillian the **jap**. Every night he prayed to **Jehovah** and asked,

"**Oy**, how much must a man take of a woman's 'she's gotta

have this and she's gotta have that!?'"

jokenik (JOKE-nick) jokester · jap (like "map") "Jewish American Princess".
jehovah (jee-HO-vah) GOD · Oy (like "boy") Oh!

"K" is for Karol the **Klutz**, who

Kvetched all day long while at work. "**Kenahura**," said Karol, "So

I **Kibbitz** all day and I like to play, does my boss have to be such a jerk?"

klutz (like "guts") clumsy person · kvetched (like "fetched") complained.
kenahura (ken-a-HAW-rah) "no evil eye" · kibbitz (KIB-its) socialize

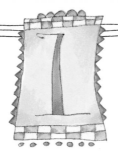

"L" is for Leonard the **lump**, who could'nt help but be such a **letz**. He loved to eat his **lox** and **latkes** and let other people pick up the checks.

lump (loomp) scoundrel • letz (like "gets") prankster • lox (like "box") smoked salmon • latkes (LOT-KUZ) potato pancakes

"M" is for Morris the **macher**, who was

just a little bit on the **meshugge** side." Such **mazel** with all

Maidlach..." cried his mother. "God forbid he should be a

Mentch, make his mother happy, and take one as his bride."

macher (MOCK-er) big shot • Meshugge (MAH-SHU-ge) crazy.
Mazel (like "nozzle") luck • maidlach (MAID-lock) young women • mentch (like "bench") giving person

"N is for Naomi the **nudnik**, who brought her parents much **nachas** in life. "So, she's a **nebbish** and her husband's a **nudj**," said her mother; "**nu**... at least she's somebody's wife!"

nudnik (NUD-nick) a bore • nachas (KNOCK-us) pride, joy •
nebbish (NEB-bish) pitiful person • nudj (NUDjeh) a pest • nu (NEW) so?

"O" is for Ozzie the **oisgeputzt** old man.

"Oy vey ihz mihr!" complained his wife; "even when I get all

oisgetzatzket, I can't look as good as he can!"

oisgeputzt (OY-geh-putzed) overdressed.
Oy Vey Ihz Mihr! (OY VEY IS ME-er) "oh! woe is me!"
oisgetzatzket (OY-get-stock-it) overadorned

"P" is for Polly the **plosher,** who was up to her

pupik in laundry. "Five kids and a **pisher** of a husband," she sighed, "how

did such a **pritzteh** end up in such a quandary ?"

plosher (like "Kosher") a braggart · pupik (PUH-pick) belly button.
pisher (like "fisher") a nobody · pritzteh (PRITZ-eh) princess

"R" is for Rose the **Rasha,** who wanted to be

very, very **Reich** one day. So, she sold her **Rugelah,** at an extremely

high price, as much as the people would pay.

rasha (RUSH-sha) evil person • reich (like "bike") rich.
rugelah (RUG-ah-lah) pastry with nuts & raisins

"S" is for Sheldon and Sadie Shmendricks, who owned their own **shmatte** store. "Together we have three sons," complained Sadie, "Sidney a **shikker**... Saul the **shnorrer**... and Sammy who's such a bore. Our **shlemiel** son Sidney married Steffie... a **shiksa** who keeps a **shmutsik** house. And our Saul married a **sheine Maidel** named Shirley, who treats him like a louse. And let's not forget our **shlump** of a son Sammy, who has no **seichel** at all. It's such a **shande** when he tells me and his father, 'Why should I get married when I'm having such a ball!?'

"**Oy Vey ihz Mihr**, and if that's not enough... to make matters worse,

my Sheldon has **shpilkes** from **shelping**

so much **shlock**... he wants to sell the store, get rid of the whole

shmeer... go to Miami... and just sit somewhere on a dock!"

shmatte (SHMOT-ta) rag • shikker (SHICK-er) drunk • shnorrer (like "snorer") moocher.
shlemiel (shleh-MEAL) born loser • shiksa (SHICK-sah) non-jewish girl.
shmutsik (SHMUTZ-ick) dirty • sheine maidel (shane-e-may-del) pretty girl.
shlump (like "bump") a drip • seichel (like "heckle") common sense •
shande (shaun-dah) a shame • Oy Vey Ihz Mihr! (OY VEY IS ME-er) "Oh! Woe is me!".
shpilkes (SHPILK-ease) can't sit still • shleping (SHLEP-ing) dragging.
shlock (like "clock") junk • shmeer (like "shear") "the whole package".

"T" is for Toby, whose life was so full of **tsouris** that she didn't know what to do. So, she asked her **tata** for some money, but instead he gave her a good **potch** on her **tuchis** and told her to grow up a year or two.

tsouris (TSOOR-iss) troubles · tata (TAH-ta) papa · potch (POTCH) a smack.
tuchis (TUCK-hiss) bottom

"U" is for young Uri, who was always **utzen** his little

sister. **"uhch"**, yelled his father, **"umbeshrien!** You're in big

trouble if I have to pull this car over, mister!"

utzen (OOTs-ing) bothering · Uhch (UHCH) oh!.
umbeshrien (CUM-be-shrey-in) God forbid!

"V" is for Victor the **veibernik**, who thought he was quite the stud. "**vey ihz mihr**," cried his mother; "enough already, with every **shiksa** he brings home, my heart, it just drops with a thud!"

veibernik (VIBE-er-nick) womanizer • veyihzmihr (VEY is Me-er) "Woe is me!". shiksa (SHICK-sah) non-jewish woman

W is for Walter, who was a little bit weird.

He liked to eat his **Wurst** and drink his **Wishniak** while sitting

in **Weisse zekelach** and shaving his beard.

wurst (worst) salami · wishniak (wish-knee-ack) cherry brandy ·
weisse zekelach (vice zeh-kle-ach) white stockings

"Y" is for Yancy the **yenta**, who was the hit of
her Mah-Jongg group. "She's such a **yachna** with a **yiddishe Kop**,"
said her best friend, "it's from her that we get all the latest scoop."

yenta (YEN-ta) gossipy woman • yachna (YOCK-neh) blabbermouth.
yiddishe Kop (YIDDISH-ah Cup) "Jewish head"

"z" is for Ziggy, the cute and lively old **zayde**.

"zindik nit," he'd tell his **zaftig** wife Zelda during

exercise class; **"zol zein**! let's get with it, baby!"

zayde (ZAY-dee) grandfather · zindik nit (ZIN-dick knit) don't complain·
zaftig (ZOFF-tig) plump · zol zein (zol zine) that's it!

glossary

alter kaker (OLL-ter cock-er): crotchety old man
awngebluzen (AWN-ge-bluz-in): bloated, literally "blown up, inflated"
awngepatshket (AWN-ge-potch-ket): cluttered, littered

bakakt (BAH-cocked): all fouled up
bubbe (BU-bee): grandmother
bubbe maises (BU-bee my-suhs): silly stories, old wives' tales
bubkes (BUB-kess): beans, nothing

chazerai (khoz-zair-EYE): "crap", junk
chazir (KHOZ-zer): pig, greedy person, a glutton
chutzpah (KHOOTS-pah): nerve, gall, "guts"
cockamamy (COCK-a-may-me): mixed-up, muddled

draykop (DRAY-cup): scatterbrain, busybody
drein a kawps: (DRAY-in a cups): annoys, confuses

edel (AY-d'l): gentle person
ek velt (ECK velt): the end of the world
eppes (EP-piss): something

farblunjet (far-BLWAN-jit): bewildered, lost
farklempt (FAH-klempt): distressed, upset, emotional
farmihsht (far-MISHED): mixed-up, confused

ganef (GON-iff): thief , swindler
gefelt (GUH-felt): satisfied
gefilte fish (ge-FILL-teh FISH): fish cakes
gelt (like "felt"): money
oy gottenyu! (OY GAWT-en-yew): "Oh, dear God!"
goy (like "boy"): non-jew, a gentile

haimisher (HAME-ish-er): warm, having friendly characteristics
hak un pak (HOCK-un-pock): everything
hakn me a chainik (HOCK-in ME A CHAN-ick): to babble, talk a great deal
hotzenklotz (HOTS-in-klotz): the sticks

iker (E-care): substance, principle
in bod (IN BUD): in the bath
ipish (IP-ish): bad odor, stench

jap (like "map"): "Jewish American Princess" (Not

really English or Yiddish but "Yinglish" — a slang term for a rich or spoiled Jewish girl.)

jehovah (jee-HO-vah): God
jokenik (JOKE-nick): jokester

kenahura (ken-a-HAW-rah): "no evil eye" (A magical phrase uttered so that what one says won't be jinxed. When said, this shows one's praises are genuine and not to be contaminated by envy.)
kibbitz (KIB-its): socialize, joke, fool around
klutz (like "guts"): clumsy person
kvetched (like "fetched"): complained

latkes (LOT-kuz): potato pancakes
letz (like "gets"): prankster
lox (like "box"): smoked salmon
lump (loomp): scoundrel, a no-good

macher (MOCK-er): big shot, an "operator"
maidlach (MAID-lock): young women
mazel (like "nozzle"): luck
mentch (like "bench"): giving person, decent person
meshugge (mah-SHU-ge): crazy

nachas (KNOCK-us): pride, joy
nebbish (NEB-bish): pitiful person, a "nothing"
nu (NEW): So? Well?

nudj (NUDjeh): a pest
nudnik (NUD-nick): a bore

oisgeputzt (OY-geh-putzed): overdressed
oisgetzatzket (OY-get-stock-it): overadorned
oy (like "boy"): Oh!
oy vey ihz mihr! (OY VEY IS ME-er): "Oh! Woe is me!"

pished (like "fished"): unrinated
pisher (like "fisher"): a nobody
plosher (like "kosher"): a braggart, a gossip
potch (like "watch"): a smack, a slap
pritzteh (PRITZ-eh): princess, prima donna
pupik (PUH-pick): belly button, navel

rasha (RUSH-sha): evil person
reich (like "bike"): rich, wealthy
rugelah (RUG-ah-lah): pastry w/ nuts & raisins

seichel (like "heckle"): common sense, judgement
shande (SHAUN-dah): a shame
sheine maidel (SHANE-e-may-del): pretty girl
shikker (SHICK-er): drunk
shiksa (SHICK-sah): non-jewish girl
shlemiel (shleh-MEAL): born loser
shleping (SHLEP-ing): dragging

shlock (like "clock"): junk, cheaply made articles

shlump (like "bump"): a drip, a wet blanket

shmatte (SHMOT-ta): rag, junk

shmeer (like "shear"): "the whole package," "the whole deal"

shmutsik (SHMUTZ-ick): dirty, soiled

shnorrer (like "snorer"): moocher, beggar

shpilkes (SHPILK-ease): can't sit still , literally "pins and needles"

tata (TAH-ta): papa, father

tsouris (TSOOR-iss): troubles, worries

tuchis (TUCK-hiss): bottom, rear end

uhch (UHCH): Oh!

umbeshrien! (UM-be-shrey-in): God forbid!

utzen (OOTS-ing): bothering, goading

veibernik (VIBE-er-nick): womanizer, lady-killer

vey ihz mihr (VEY Is ME-er): "Woe is me!"

weisse zekelach (Vice ZEH-kle-ach): white stockings

wishniak (WISH-knee-ack): cherry brandy

wurst (WORST): salami

yachna (YOCK-neh): blabbermouth

yenta (YEN-ta): gossipy woman

yiddishe kop: (YIDDISH-ah CUP): "Jewish head" (Someone who knows their stuff, someone who is full of Jewish knowledge.)

zaftig (ZOFF-tig): plump, buxom

zayde (ZAY-dee): grandfather

zindik nit (ZIN-dick knit): don't complain

zol zein (ZOL - ZINE) That's it!

references

Jacobs, Sidney J., *The Jewish Word Book,* Jonathan David Publishers, Middle Village, NY, 1982.

Kogos, Fred, *A Dictionary of Yiddish Slang & Idioms,* Citadel Press, New York, NY, 1993.

Rosten, Leo, *The Joys of Yiddish,* Pocket Books, New York, NY, 1968.

Rosten, Leo, *The Joys of Yinglish,* Plume, New York , NY, 1990.